HAPKIDO

The author applies a jumping double front kick during the filming of
The Trial of Billy Jack.

HAPKIDO
KOREAN ART OF SELF-DEFENSE
by Bong Soo Han

Library of Congress Catalog Card Number: 74-15500
ISBN 0-89750-011-3
Twenty-seventh printing 2002

Graphic Design by Sunny Kim

OHARA 🔟 PUBLICATIONS, INCORPORATED
SANTA CLARITA, CALIFORNIA

DEDICATION

My special thanks to Richard Friske, whose excellent photography enabled me to complete this book. His professional attitude made our working hours a pleasant experience.

ACKNOWLEDGMENT

Master Bong Soo Han approaches Hapkido as a complete system of self-defense that offers a philosophy for life. He shows the Hapkido student a path to physical well-being as well as the psychological flexibility to deal with difficult people in any setting. Hapkido's non-resistant, circular, flowing techniques can disarm someone who is verbally abusive as easily as an attacker on the street. All who know him have benefited from his generous wisdom, as better martial artists and as healthier people.

Speaking for all the students who have learned so much from Master Bong Soo Han's teaching, I extend my most heartfelt thanks.

Robert W. Sweitzer, Ph.D.

CONTENTS

ABOUT THE AUTHOR

The world's foremost practitioner of Hapkido is Master Bong Soo Han. He has studied and refined this powerful Korean martial art form for more than 40 years. He currently holds the rank of ninth degree black belt, and is chairman of the International Hapkido Federation.

Although Master Han first introduced Hapkido into the United States in 1967, mass exposure to the general public did not come until the motion picture *Billy Jack* filled the nation's theaters in 1971. In this film, Master Han gained critical acclaim for creating and staging some of the most breathtaking and realistic fight sequences that have ever graced the silver screen.

In the ensuing years, Master Han has choreographed, doubled, produced, and starred in numerous films, including *The Trial of Billy Jack, Kentucky Fried Movie, Kill the Golden Goose, Force Five,* and *Presidio.*

Master Bong Soo Han has been the subject of numerous martial arts magazine cover stories and is a member of the *Black Belt* magazine Hall of Fame (1978). He operates his own instructional school in Santa Monica, California, and tours the world lecturing on and demonstrating Hapkido, the Art of Coordinated Power.

PREFACE

The purpose of this book is to introduce the student to Hapkido in the clearest terms, with special emphasis on the basic techniques and principles of the art. Nothing can take the place of actual practice of the physical art, and it is suggested that you seek the opportunity to see a demonstration of Hapkido, or study the techniques in a class.

This book can be used to organize your own workouts, typically beginning with all the warm-up and stretching exercises, followed by the basic kicks and punches. Once these basics are completed, select a specific defense against a punch or a defense against a kick, and practice it for several days before going on to the next technique. Repeat this sequence for several weeks until the techniques become reflexive, so that you will not have to think, but only react to an attack.

HISTORY OF HAPKIDO

Thirteen centuries ago, the people of Korea were unified under the sovereignty of King Chin-Heung. But in the years to follow, their country was torn apart by wars and insurrections. During the Silla dynasty, it was felt that the security of many lay in the strength, physical and mental endurance of a select few. Each king gathered about him an elite group of young noblemen—knights who were highly disciplined, adhered to a strict code of ethics and were extremely proficient in the art of killing with their bare hands.

The martial art of these men, who called themselves Hwarangdo, reigned for two hundred years.

During the Yi dynasty, the kings initiated various cultural arts. As the arts began to flourish, violence decreased. Painting, sculpturing, and writing replaced the art of fighting. Those who followed the old ways were banished and forced to retreat into monastic orders secluded high in the mountains of Korea. Thereafter, the martial arts were to be practiced only in secret.

For 500 years, these secret art forms were practiced and refined by devoted monks. Many of them developed their own styles of fighting, the most effective and devastating of which was the form called Tae-kyon. This is primarily the martial art of kicking. So fantastic and so powerful were its techniques that even today, only a handful of men have mastered it. One such man is the well-known Master Bong Soo Han, instructor of Hapkido.

Hapkido is a martial art of great depth. It does not rely on physical strength to subdue an aggressor, but rather a knowledge of body mechanics and movement. Hapkido incorporates the kicking techniques of Tae-kyon, joint locking, throwing and pressure points as well as the use of internal strength.

After years of personal development, Master Han has initiated a few refinements in Hapkido, making it an art which is attracting considerable attention today. His refinements are included in this text.

PHILOSOPHY OF HAPKIDO

The word, *Hap-ki-do*, literally translated, means coordination, power and way. *Hap* is coordination, *ki* denotes the essence of power, and *do* means the art, or method. Hapkido, the art of coordinated power.

The practitioner of Hap-ki-do learns to apply all three of the principles in mastering his art. Central, and most important, is ki, the essence of the power. It is gained by joining the mind and the body into one spiritual and physical unit.

As he begins to recognize his ki and to develop unity in mind and body, the student is taught basic techniques—blocks, punches, kicks and throws. From that point, he must learn to coordinate his new-found abilities into free-flowing power or energy.

There are three basic skills to be learned:

1. Non-resistance. Meet forces with minimum force to deflect and not clash with an adversary's power.

2. Circular motion, countering and attacking.

3. The "Water Principle." Total penetration of an enemy's defenses.

Non-resistance is a characteristic of Hapkido and one of the major areas where the art differs from its more traditional karate cousins. For example, in defending against a powerfully thrown punch, the Hapkido practitioner would never step inside his opponent's area of greatest momentum and block with a hard right angle thrust. Instead, he would avoid a direct confrontation by stepping to the outside to parry the punch with a soft circular motion of the arm and hand. Once the power has been diverted, he would then be free to attack his opponent's exposed side.

The same circle which allows the Hapkido practitioner to flow from one motion to the next without interruption, provides an unbroken line of continuous motion, power and energy.

The circular method of attacking is the principal method of combat employed by predatory animals. An example would be a cat stalking and and attacking its prey with its characteristic circular patterns.

The Hapkido practitioner uses circular patterns to gain momentum for executing the techniques in a natural and free-flowing manner. Straight but jerky movements are extremely difficult to redirect once the power has been unleashed. However, by employing the principle of the circle, the momentum can be changed from a frontal to a lateral motion, etc., by simply altering the axis of the circle. Therefore, one can quite easily and freely move from a circular pattern to another. It is in this manner that Hapkido karate is coordinated.

The "Water Principle" is best described if one pictures the quiet, direct strength in free-flowing water. As the flowing stream penetrates and surrounds its obstructions and as the dripping water eventually penetrates the stone, so does the Hapkido strength flow in and through its opponents.

TAN-JON BREATHING

WHAT IS TAN-JON?

Dan Tiyan

A small portion of the abdominal region is referred to as the *Tan Jon*.

To locate the Tan Jon, measure two inches directly below the navel. Using this point as the center, form a square around it with two inches to each side. This is Tan Jon.

It is believed that all physical energy in man originates in this area called Tan Jon.

This energy developed in Tan Jon is referred to as the ki (pronounced "key").

chi

CONCENTRATION

The importance of concentration in Hapkido cannot be over-emphasized. Karate is more than just physical training. It also involves mental discipline, of which concentration is an integral part. Without it, Hapkido can never be mastered. It gives you power, focus, precision, continuity, speed, alertness, awareness and strength.

True concentration is totally focusing one's attention on something to the exclusion of all things that are irrelevant.

There are several methods of developing concentration:

1. When relaxing, select a technique and concentrate on it for several minutes without allowing any other thought to enter your mind.

2. When practicing a technique or exercise, concentrate on every movement before and during its execution.

3. When watching others performing Karate techniques; focus your attention on their movements. Do not let your attention wander or be diverted.

When you mentally imagine an action in your mind, see its execution in perfection. Your physical actions are a reflection of the images in your mind.

One of the best ways to study a person is to watch his movements. If his mind is uneasy, restless, erratic and unsteady, his physical actions will be the same. Lack of concentration is indicative of a weak mind.

Concentration is a disciplined control of the mind and body.

THE PURPOSE OF
ABDOMINAL BREATHING

There are several reasons for utilizing the abdominal breathing method.

1. Concentration—One must be able to exclude all irrelevant thoughts and activity. Full concentration on a singular activity accelerates learning and muscle coordination.

2. Patience—Due to the inherent complexity of Hapkido karate and the amount of time and practice necessary to develop the proper coordination, one must have patience. Many repetitions of slow, deliberate abdominal breathing movements which are physically strenuous help one to develop this patience.

3. Blood Circulation—This exercise temporarily increases blood flow helping to cleanse the body and improve overall circulation.

4. Strength—All power in karate is derived from the Tan Jon. Knowing how to control and use this ki (energy), one can develop tremendous strength.

5. The goal of a true Hapkido karate student is to be pure in body, mind and spirit. Proper abdominal breathing is an important step toward obtaining this goal.

Front View

Front View

Side View

Side View

THE METHOD OF ABDOMINAL BREATHING
(Tan-Jon-Ho-Heup-Bup)

(1) Begin by standing with your feet spread slightly wider than your shoulders, your back straight, your elbows at your sides and your head up. At this point, take a slow deep breath, pushing the air down into the Tan Jon area, and hold it as you tighten your abdominal muscles. (2) From this position, bend your knees so that you squat slightly and begin to open your hands and spread your fingers. (3 & 4) Raise your arms upward

3   **4**

Front View   Front View

Side View   Side View

slowly until your hands are at eye level. Imagine a big rock in front of you and, using your fingertips, slowly remove this rock by pushing your hands forward and upward. At this point, you should feel the ki (energy) flowing from the Tan Jon up through your body into your arms, hands and spine.

After your hands have reached eye level, you may lower them slowly to their original position, exhaling as you do this.

Do as many repetitions of this abdominal breathing exercise as you can before going on to any warm-up exercises. More advanced breathing techniques will be explained in the advanced Hapkido volumes.

STRIKING
POINTS

This section is intended to illustrate the various parts of your hands, feet and knees that can be used as weapons against an opponent. They usually are marked by points where your skin covers a bone with as little cushion as possible. Before going on to the subsequent sections on technique, be sure that you have become well acquainted with your striking areas.

STRIKING AREAS OF THE FEET

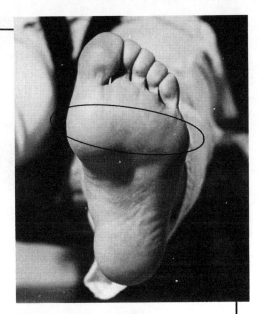

THE BALL OF THE FOOT
(Ahp-Bahl-Keum-Chi)

This striking point, located between the arch and the toes of your foot, provides you with a powerful weapon. When using this area for strikes, be sure to curl your toes back, as seen in the examples.

APPLICATION A: A front kick to the midsection.
APPLICATION B: A roundhouse kick to the jaw.

Application A

Application B

17

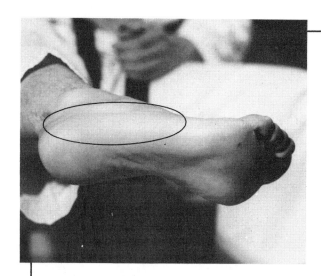

KNIFE FOOT
(Chok-Do)

This striking point is located on the outside edge, or "blade" of your foot. The knife foot extends from your heel up to, but not including the ball of your foot. Your foot has to be curled inward toward your inside ankle in order to expose this edge for kicking, as can be seen in the example.

APPLICATION: A side kick to the opponent's midsection.

Application

BACK OF THE HEEL
(Bahl-Deet-Cheuk)

This striking point is located along the bone area between the bottom of your heel and your achilles tendon. It is most often used in kicks which are coming downward or backward, as can be seen in the examples.

APPLICATION A: A spinning wheel kick.
APPLICATION B: A downward heel kick.

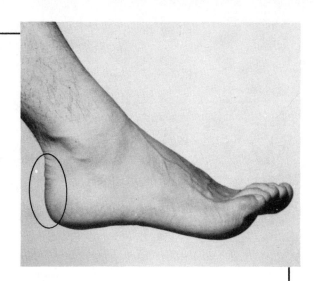

Application A

Application B

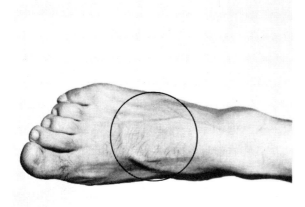

INSTEP
(Bahl-Deung)

This striking point is located along the bony top of your foot between your ankle and your toes.

APPLICATION: A front snap kick to the groin.

Application

BOTTOM OF THE HEEL
(Deet-Bahl-Deum-Chi)

This striking point consists of the bony heel portion along the bottom of your foot. It is most often used in kicks with thrust rather than snap, as seen in the example.

APPLICATION: A step-by-step view of the front heel kick being initiated against an opponent's mid-section.

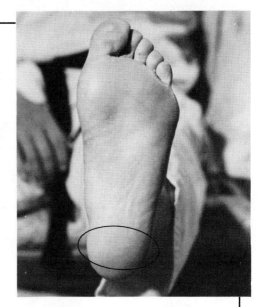

Application

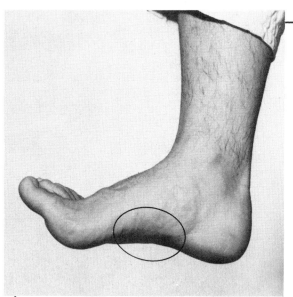

ARCH or
INSIDE EDGE
OF FOOT
(Ahn-Chok-Bahl)

This striking point is located along the inside lower edge of your foot between the heel and the ball, and directly below the instep. It is used mainly in kicks at lower targets, as seen in the example.

APPLICATION: An inside foot sweep.

Application

STRIKING AREAS OF THE HANDS

FOREFIST (Chung-Kwon)

This striking point is located along the knuckles of your fist. It is on the same side of your fist as are your fingers, between the first and second knuckles.

APPLICATION: A right forward punch to the midsection.

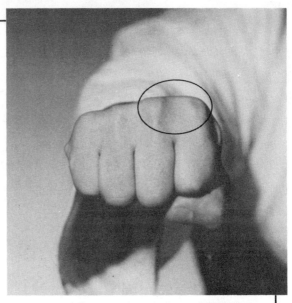

Application

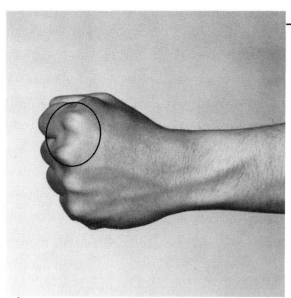

BACKFIST
(Ye-Kwon)

This striking point is located on the back side of the bottom knuckles of your index and middle fingers.

APPLICATION: A right outward backfist to the temple.

Application

BOTTOMFIST
(Yoo-Kwon)

This striking point is located along the back heel of your fist, between the lower part of your last knuckle and the protruding bone of your hand, just above your wrist.

APPLICATION: A downward bottomfist strike to the head.

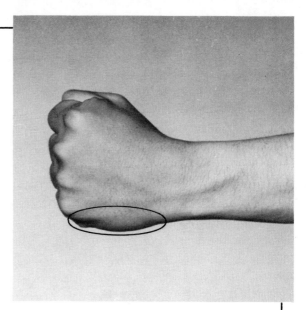

Application

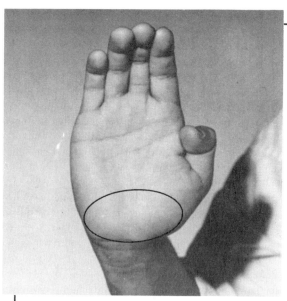

PALM HEEL
(Chang-Kwon)

This striking point is located along the muscle and bone area at the base of your palm. You may flex this area by bringing your fingers tightly together at the knuckles and curling your thumb inward.

APPLICATION: An upward palm heel strike to the jaw.

Application

KNIFE HAND
(Soo-Do)

This striking point is located along the outer edge of your hand between the base of your small finger and the bone protruding from your hand adjacent to the wrist joint. You may flex this area by bringing your fingers tightly together at the knuckles and curling your thumb inward.

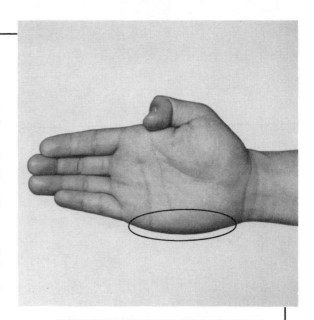

APPLICATION A: A right inward knife hand strike to the head.
APPLICATION B: A right downward knife hand strike to the neck.
APPLICATION C: A right outward knife hand strike to the jaw.

Application B

Application A

Application C

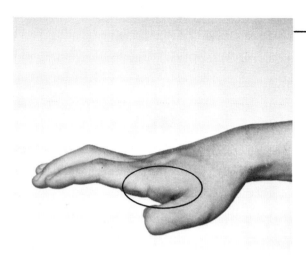

INNER EDGE
(Yuk-Soo-Do)

This striking point is located along the inside area of the hand between the bottom knuckles of the thumb and index finger. The area may be flexed by holding your fingers taut and slightly bent with your thumb curled inward.

APPLICATION: A right inner edge strike to the temple.

Application

INSIDE
CIRCLE RIDGE
(Won-Yuk-Soo-Do)

This striking point is located along the fleshy area between the tip of your thumb and the first knuckle of your index finger.

APPLICATION: A right inside circle ridge to the throat.

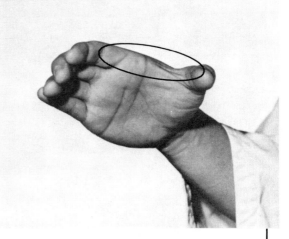

Application

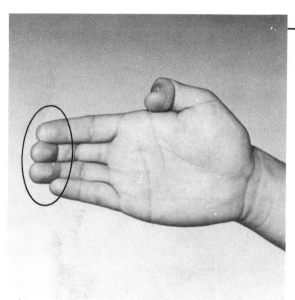

SPEAR FINGERS
(Kwan-Soo)

This striking point is located at the tips of your four fingers. Their striking power may be enhanced by slightly bending and flexing these fingers while curling your thumb inward.

APPLICATION: A right spear finger strike to the solar plexus.

Application

STRIKING AREAS OF THE ELBOW

INSIDE ELBOW (Pahl-Keum-Chi)

This striking point is located at the point of the elbow where the bone protrudes.

APPLICATION A: A right inside elbow strike to the solar plexus.

APPLICATION B: An upward right inside elbow strike to the chin.

APPLICATION C: An upward right inside elbow strike to the jaw.

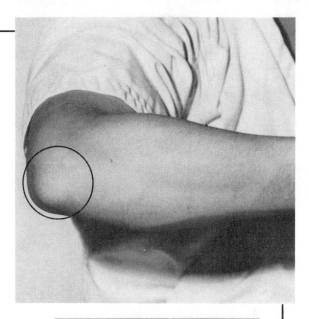

Application B

Application A

Application C

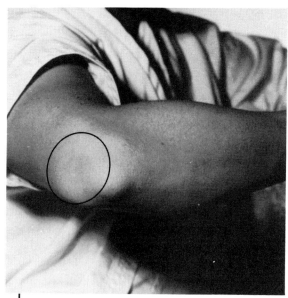

OUTSIDE ELBOW
(Pahl-Keum-Chi)

This striking point is located behind the point of the elbow in the hard, flat area.

APPLICATION: A right downward outside elbow strike to the back.

Application

STRIKING AREAS OF THE KNEE

FRONT KNEE (Moo-Roop)

This striking area is located at the upper part of your bent knee at the very top of your kneecap.

APPLICATION A: A right upward knee strike to the chin.
APPLICATION B: A right inward knee strike to the solar plexus.

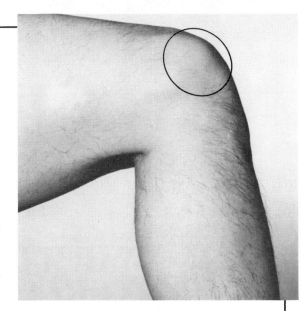

Application A

Application B

WARM-UP EXERCISES

Although it may seem a pointless ritual to you, warming up before each workout will prevent such bothersome injuries as pulled muscles. Warm-ups are also designed to build strength and endurance in your joints and muscles as they limber up.

This is particularly important in light of Hapkido's heavy emphasis on kicking. One must become proficient in the art of stretching, and follow the warm-up routine daily, in order to remain in good physical condition.

Front View

OPEN STANCE
EXERCISE I

(1) Begin by standing erect with your hands at your sides and your feet spread to just over shoulder-width. (2) Bend

Front View

Side View

forward and touch the floor with the palms of your hands without moving your legs or bending your knees.

Side View

OPEN STANCE
EXERCISE II

(1) Begin by standing erect with your arms extended straight out to the side and your feet spread to just over shoulder-width. (2) Bend over without moving your legs or bending your knees and touch your right hand to the floor in front of your

left foot. Your other arm should be extended straight upward. (3) Rotate your torso as you straighten it and bend over again, this time placing your left palm on the floor in front of your right foot. (4) Return to the starting position.

OPEN STANCE
EXERCISE III

(1) Begin by standing erect with your arms held slightly in front of your thighs and your feet spread to just over shoulder-width. (2) Without moving your legs or bending your knees, bend over at your hips and touch the floor between your feet with the tips of your fingers.

(3) Bend back so that you are once again erect and hold your arms aloft, leaning your trunk to the left as far as you can go. (4) Bend back into an erect position, holding your arms aloft and (5) lean your trunk to the right as far as you can go.

Front View

CLOSED STANCE
EXERCISE I

(1) Begin by standing erect with your hands at your sides and your feet together. (2) Bend forward at the hips without moving

Front View

Side View

your legs or bending your knees and touch the floor with the palms of your hands.

Side View

LEG STRETCH EXERCISE I

(1) Begin by standing erect with your arms at your sides and your feet spread to about two shoulder-widths. (2) Slide your left leg straight out to the side as you squat down on your right leg. You may support yourself by placing your right hand on your right knee, while you make the most of the stretch by pressing down on your left knee with your left hand. (3) Pull your left leg back in beneath your buttocks and perform the same procedure with your right leg, extending it and stretching it.

LEG STRETCH
EXERCISE II

(1) Begin by standing erect with your hands at your sides and your feet spread about two shoulder-widths. (2) Turn your torso to the right and squat down on your right leg as you simultaneously slide your left leg straight out to the side. You may anchor yourself by grasping your right knee with both hands. (3) Bring your left leg in and squat on it as you extend your right leg straight out to the side. Rock on your extended leg to be sure you are gaining the maximum from this stretching exercise.

SITTING LEG SPREAD EXERCISE

(1) Begin by sitting on the floor with your legs spread apart as far as you can spread them and your hands resting palm down on the floor. (2) Grasp your calves with your hands and slowly lower yourself until you touch your forehead to the floor.

SITTING LEG FORWARD EXERCISE

(1) Begin in the split position, sitting on the floor with your left leg extended in front of you and your right leg behind you. (2) Without bending your knees, lower your torso until your forehead touches your forward leg. (3 & 4) Repeat this exercise using the right leg forward.

SIT-UP I

(1) Begin by assuming the classic sit-up position, sitting on the floor with your legs extended together and your hands behind your neck. (2) Slowly lower your upper body until you are near the floor. (3) Using only your stomach muscles, raise your upper body until your head is over your knees.

Straight sit-ups may also be performed with your hands at your sides to grasp your feet when you sit forward, as in pictures (1 & 2).

SIT-UP II

(1) Begin in the sit-up position with your legs straight and together and your hands locked behind your head. (2) Bend your upper torso to the right at a point just above your hips, being sure you do not move your legs or bend your knees. (3) Bend your upper torso to the left, as far as you can go.

SIT-UP III

(1) Begin by assuming the classic sit-up position with your hands locked behind your neck. (2, 3 & 4) Without moving your legs or bending your knees, begin rotating your torso in circular motions, first to your left side, then around behind and to your right side, and finally forward over your legs.

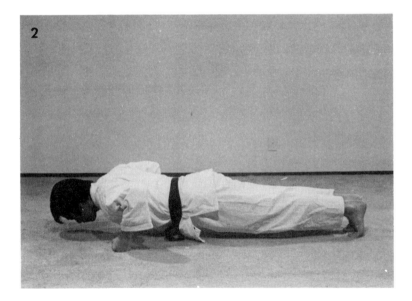

PUSH-UP I

(1) Begin by assuming the classic push-up position, with your back straight and your weight resting on the balls of your feet. The only exception is that you will be pushing up with the knuckles of each hand. (2) Slowly lower yourself until you have almost touched the floor and raise yourself up again.

PUSH-UP II

(1) Begin by assuming the classic push-up position, only you will be pushing up on all of your fingertips. (2) Gradually lower your body until it almost comes in contact with the floor and raise yourself up to the starting position again.

Front View

Front View

PUSH-UP III

(1) Begin by suspending your body in a prone position, and rest your weight on the palms of your hands and on the soles of your feet, which are spread about two shoulder-widths. Be sure to keep your knees straight. (2) Gradually lower your upper body to a point just short of touch-

Front View

Side View

ing the floor. Be sure to keep your legs straight and your posterior up. (3) Raise your upper body and lower your posterior to a point just short of touching the floor, and follow through by raising your entire body back to the original position of this exercise.

Side View

Side View

Front View

KICK STRETCH I

(1) Begin by spreading your legs to about a shoulder-and-a-half-width, with your right leg positioned in front of your left. (2) From this

Front View

Side View

position, kick with your left leg as high as you possibly can. Repeat this process, kicking with both legs.

Side View

Front View

KICK STRETCH II

(1) Begin by assuming a left forward stance, your legs spread to about a shoulder-and-a-half-width. (2) Kick your rear leg (the right, in this case), as far up and to the side as you

Front View

Side View

possibly can. One trick which may help you in this kick stretching is to remember to twist your hips away from the kick and lower your torso.

Side View

BASIC FIGHTING POSITION

Front View

There are a number of fighting positions which may be employed by the expert in Hapkido, but since this book is primarily to be concerned with the beginning student, we will deal only with the single position which is most often used when fighting or executing the techniques.

The position goes as follows:

(1) Stand erect with your feet parallel to one another and spread to a single shoulder-width. Keep your arms at your sides. (2) Slide one foot straight back (the right foot, in this case), being sure to maintain the same distance between your feet. (3) Turn your rear foot slightly to the side so that it is at a 45-degree angle to the other foot. Distribute your weight equally on each foot, and bend your knees slightly. Turn your shoulders slightly to the side, your right shoulder turned toward your right foot and vice versa. Raise the arm on the same side as your forward leg (the left arm, in this case) and hold it forward at chest level. Your other arm should be held closer into your body at about stomach level.

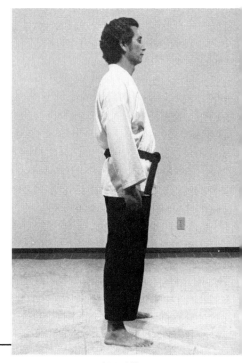

Side View

Front View

Front View

Side View

Side View

PUNCHING
AND
STRIKING

In the Hapkido system, punching and striking techniques comprise a smaller part of the defensive and offensive counter-attack techniques than does the kicking, but are very important if you expect to become proficient in breaking an attack. The following section will deal with the various punches and strikes common to the Hapkido system. They will be presented and classified according to the striking point used in each maneuver. Practice each technique in the order it is presented to you, step-by-step, until your motions become fluid and the entire technique becomes a single movement.

The punching and striking techniques offered in this section will facilitate your ability for in-fighting, and will help you keep your opponent off guard as an alternative to kicking.

HAND STRIKES

FOREFIST

(1) Begin by assuming the basic fighting position. (2) Throw a punch at the target with your back hand, remembering to twist it in a corkscrew motion. Your other hand should be brought back to your waist simultaneously in a corkscrew motion. (3) At the completion of the punch, your shoulder should remain perpendicular to the ground, and not extended beyond your neck. The power of this strike should come from the speed with which it is thrown and from the slight twisting of your hips.

Front View

Side View

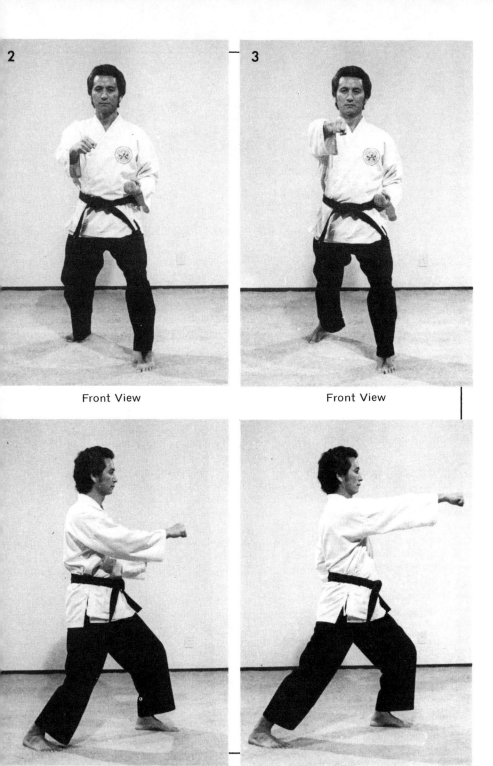

Front View

Front View

Side View

Side View

BACKFIST

(1) Begin by assuming the basic fighting position. (2 & 3) Bend your forward arm in at the elbow and strike out with it, hitting the target with a backfist.

(4) When the strike is completed, your body should be leaning slightly toward the target and your arm should be extended, but not straight.

Front View

Front View

Side View

Side View

VERTICAL KNIFE HAND

(1) Begin by assuming the basic fighting position. (2) Make knife hands and raise your rear hand to a position just above the shoulder, even with

3

Front View

4

Front View

Side View

Side View

the head. (3 & 4) Strike with a circular motion and be sure to follow through in order to get the maximum power from your blow.

Front View	Front View

Side View

Side View

HORIZONTAL KNIFE HAND

(1) Begin by assuming the basic fighting position. (2) Make a knife hand with your back fist and raise it to about shoulder-height. (3 & 4) Strike

3

4

Front View

Front View

Side View

Side View

with a circular motion, being sure the arc is more horizontal, and come across in front of your head with your arm extended.

REVERSE KNIFE HAND

(1) Begin by assuming the basic fighting position. (2) Make knife hands and cock your front arm (the right, in this case), bringing it back behind your head, holding it away from

your body. (3 & 4) Strike forward in a circular and horizontal motion, remembering to follow through for the maximum of power.

Front View

Front View

Side View

Side View

INNER EDGE

(1) Begin by assuming the basic fighting position, making knife hands. (2) Lean forward on your front leg and extend your rear arm out to the side. (3 & 4) Strike in a circular and horizontal motion, using your inner edge

3

4

Front View

Front View

Side View

Side View

hand as the striking point, and remembering to follow through with the strike for power.

SPEAR FINGER

(1) Begin by assuming the basic fighting position, making knife hands. (2) Lean forward on your front leg and begin to make a strike with a rear hand. (3) When the strike is complete, your arm should be fully extended with the tips of your fingers being the striking points.

INSIDE CIRCLE RIDGE

(1) Begin by assuming the basic fighting position. (2 & 3) Strike with your rear hand, thrusting your inside circle ridge forward in the direction of the opponent's throat.

1

PALM HEEL

(1) Begin by assuming the basic fighting position. (2 & 3) Strike with your rear hand, thrusting the heel of your palm at the target, as you lean forward on your front leg.

Front View

Side View

2

Front View

3

Front View

Side View

Side View

HORIZONTAL BOTTOM FIST

(1) Begin by assuming the basic fighting position. (2 & 3) Extend your rear hand out to the side, with the palm of your fist pointing upward. Be sure to bring your other fist

back into your hip with the palm upward. (4) Strike across in a circular and horizontal motion, using the bottom of your fist as the contact point.

VERTICAL BOTTOM FIST

(1) Begin by assuming the basic fighting position. (2) Extend your rear arm out to the side and bend it up at the elbow so that your rear fist is level with your cheekbone. Remember to

lean forward on your front leg. (3 & 4) Strike in a circular and downward vertical motion, using the bottom fist as your point of contact.

1

2

Front View   Front View

Side View   Side View

ELBOW STRIKES

HORIZONTAL ELBOW

(1) Begin by assuming the basic fighting position. (2 & 3) Keeping your rear fist level and near your rear shoulder, raise your rear arm so that the

3 — **4**

Front View

Front View

Side View

Side View

elbow is in line with the shoulder. (4) Strike with the point of your elbow by rotating your arm at the shoulder in a horizontal circle.

REVERSE ELBOW

(1) Begin by assuming the basic fighting position. (2) Lean forward on your front leg and cock your front arm back across your

chest, keeping it away from your body. (3 & 4) Strike outward with an outside elbow in a circular and horizontal motion.

Front View   Front View

Side View   Side View

UPWARD ELBOW

(1) Begin by assuming the basic fighting position. (2 & 3) Lean forward on your front foot and begin to strike upward with your elbow. Be sure to keep your fist near your face as you raise your elbow by the shoulder

3

Front View

4

Front View

Side View

Side View

joint. (4) Complete the strike snapping your elbow upward at the shoulder.

DOWNWARD ELBOW

(1) Begin by assuming the basic fighting position. (2) Lean forward on your front leg and raise your rear elbow up at the

shoulder. (3) Strike downward with the outer
elbow, lowering your
other hand simultaneously
to add power to the blow.

1

KNEE STRIKES

FRONT KNEE

(1) Begin with your feet positioned in the basic fighting stance, and lean forward on your front foot. Hold your arms out in front of you, as though you were grasping an opponent by the shoulders. (2 & 3) Simultaneously pull down with your hands and raise your knee upward, making a theoretical strike at the opponent's upper body or head.

Front View

Side View

2

Front View

3

Front View

Side View

Side View

Front View

ANGULAR KNEE

(1) Begin by assuming the basic fighting position. (2) Raise your rear leg upward and slightly outward. (3) Strike with the front of the knee after you have brought it up and around in a circular motion. This can be an effective move for in-fighting when you wish to deliver a medium blow.

Side View

2

Front View

3

Front View

Side View

Side View

BLOCKS

The Hapkido system implements blocks to deflect the strikes of an attacker, rather than trying to stop them directly. Most of the Hapkido blocks are performed with only one of two possible points of contact. As seen in the illustration, these contact points are either the bony part on the outside of the wrist area, or the bony part on the inside of the wrist area. Your forearm is the most effective part of your body for blocking.

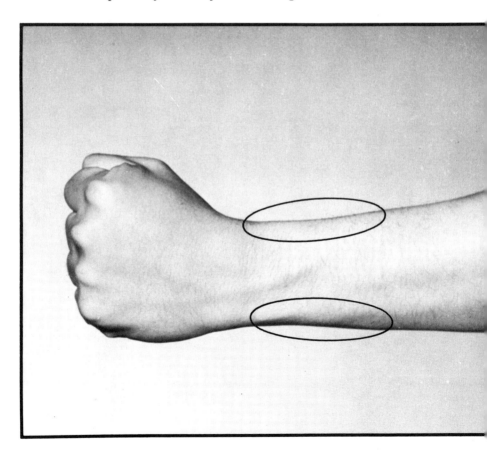

UPWARD FOREARM DEFLECTION

(1) Begin by assuming the basic fighting position. (2 & 3) Twist your hips toward your forward leg and move your rear arm upward at the shoulder and outward at the elbow. At the completion of the forearm deflection, your blocking arm should be perpendicular with the floor and your fist should be even with your forehead.

| 1 | 2 |

Front View   Front View

Side View   Side View

HORIZONTAL FOREARM DEFLECTION

(1) Begin by assuming the basic fighting position. (2) Lean forward on your front leg and raise your forward arm until it is perpendicular with the floor and even with your eyes. (3 & 4) From this position, move your arm laterally in front of you until you have made contact with the back of

Front View   Front View

Side View   Side View

your forearm. At the completion of the block, your fist should be even with your eyes and perpendicular with the floor and your opposite shoulder.

LEFT SIDE FOREARM DEFLECTION

(1) Begin by assuming the basic fighting position. (2) Step forward with your rear leg while you simultaneously lower your forward arm with the fist pointing outward and downward. (3) Complete the block in a circular motion with the palm of your fist pointing inward and your right leg planted about two shoulder-lengths from the left at a 45-degree outward angle.

RIGHT SIDE FOREARM DEFLECTION

(1) Begin by assuming the basic fighting position. (2 & 3) Step outward to the side with your front leg and block outward and downward with your right forearm. Perform the block with a circular motion. Finishing it with your right arm extended and your fist pointing down and away from your body at a 45-degree angle.

KICKS

BASIC KICKS

Perhaps the most powerful blows the human body can deliver are executed by the kick. When the ability to use the leg and foot as weapons is refined, kicking becomes an awesome means of counterattack.

The following section forms the backbone of hapkido kicking techniques. This section should become completely familiar to you before you attempt to learn any of the more advanced kicks. Practice each kick, step-by-step, keeping an eye on their applications. Be sure you are using the proper striking point. After a certain amount of practice on each kick, your technique will become more fluid and you will be able to kick in a single, fluid motion. Only then should you proceed to the more advanced kicks.

Front View   Front View

Side View   Side View

FRONT KICK

(1) Begin by assuming the basic fighting position. (2) Lean forward on your front leg. (3 & 4) Bring your rear leg up to waist level by bending your knee and snap your foot forward, hitting the target with the ball of

3

Front View

4

Front View

Side View

Side View

your foot. When the kick is completed, your leg should follow the identical path back to its starting position.

Front View

INSTEP TO GROIN KICK

(1) Begin by assuming the basic fighting position. (2) Bend your rear knee and bring it forward until it is level with your waist and parallel to the ground. (3) Snap your foot upward, pointing your toes so that you strike up into the groin area with your instep. Immediately upon completion of this kick, your leg should snap back into its original position, following the same route.

Side View

2

Front View

3

Front View

Side View

Side View

Front View

Front View

Side View

Side View

BOTTOM HEEL KICK

(1) Begin by assuming the basic fighting position. (2) Bring your rear leg up above your waist by bending your knee forward. (3 & 4) Kick your foot upward and bend it back toward your body so that the heel is

3

Front View

4

Front View

Side View

Side View

exposed at the point of contact. You should bend your anchor knee slightly and lean back in order to get the proper elevation in this kick.

SWEEP KICK

(1) Begin by assuming the basic fighting position. (2) Lean forward on your front foot and begin to slide your rear foot forward and outward. (3) In a

circular motion, sweep your rear leg around in front of you, as if to sweep your opponent's front leg out from under him.

| 1 | 2 |

Front View   Front View

Side View   Side View

SIDE KICK

(1) Begin by assuming the basic fighting position. (2) Lean straight up on your front leg and raise your rear leg by bending the knee. (3) As your rear knee becomes level with your waist, immediately pivot your anchor foot 180 degrees to the outside and allow your hips to turn with this move. (4)

Front View   Front View

Side View   Side View

Lean your upper body backward with your shoulders held perpendicular to the ground while you simultaneously kick your lifted leg out sideways and strike the target with a knife foot.

Front View

Front View

Side View

Side View

ROUNDHOUSE KICK

(1) Begin by assuming the basic fighting position. (2) Lean straight up on your front leg and raise your rear leg by bending the knee. (3) Continue raising your rear knee until it becomes level with your chest while you simultaneously pivot your anchor foot 180 degrees to the outside. (4)

3 **4**

Front View   Front View

Side View   Side View

Lean your upper body slightly backward and, in a circular motion, bring your foot around to kick the target with either the instep or the ball of your foot.

ADVANCED KICKS

This section will probably present the greatest problems to a hapkido student. It requires a great deal of patience, a determination to learn through constant practice, good coordination, and most of all, a working knowledge of the basic kicks offered in the preceding section.

Do not allow yourself to be discouraged if you cannot master such techniques as the "spinning heel kick," etc., at the outset. Practice diligently and they will come in time. The most important thing is to concentrate on each individual step in these kicking techniques and be sure you have perfected each step before combining all of them into a single fluid kicking motion. Once you have mastered the advanced Hapkido kicks, you may go on to the next section, which illustrates how they are to be applied in given situations.

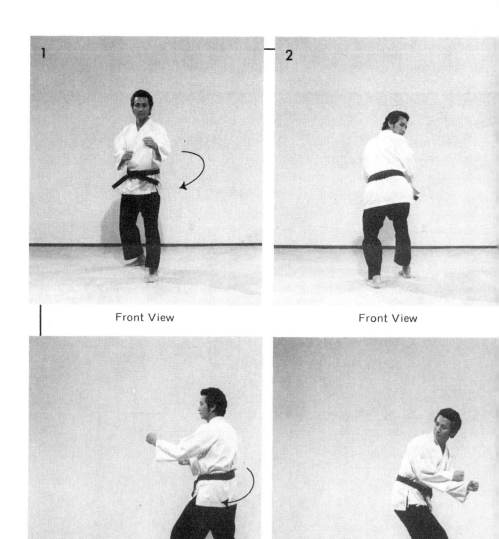

Front View	Front View
Side View	Side View

PIVOTING BACK SIDE KICK

(1) Begin by assuming the basic fighting position. (2) Pivoting on your front leg, turn 180 degrees to your right and keep the target in sight by peering over your shoulder. (3) Lean your upper body forward and raise your rear leg (the right, in this case), being sure to keep your target in

3   4

Front View   Front View

Side View   Side View

sight. (4) Bend your upper body down with your shoulders perpendicular
to the ground and execute a side kick, striking with the knife edge of your
foot.

PIVOTING BACK SIDE KICK APPLICATION

Front View

Front View

Front View

SPINNING HEEL KICK

(1) Begin by assuming the basic fighting position. (2) Pivoting on your front leg, turn 180 degrees to your right and keep the target in sight by peering over your shoulder. (3) Lean your upper body to

Front View

Front View

Side View

Side View

Side View

the side and, making sure to keep the target in sight, extend your rear leg (the right, in this case) straight out to the side. (4 & 5) Follow through with a heel kick, executed in a circular motion.

Side View

Side View

SPINNING HEEL KICK APPLICATION

Front View

JUMPING SIDE KICK

(1) Begin by assuming the basic fighting position. (2) Begin a single jump forward by pushing off with your rear foot, leaving the ground and landing first on your front foot. (3) As soon as your rear foot lands, execute a side kick, striking your target with a knife foot.

Side View

2

Front View

3

Front View

Side View

Side View

JUMPING SIDE KICK APPLICATION

129

Front View   Front View

Application

JUMPING ROUNDHOUSE KICK

(1) Begin by assuming the basic fighting position. (2) Begin a single jump forward by pushing off with your rear foot, leaving the ground and landing first on your front foot. (3) As soon as your rear foot lands, execute a

Front View

roundhouse kick, making contact with either the instep or the ball of your foot.

1

Front View

2

Front View

3

Front View

JUMPING HEEL KICK

(1) Begin by assuming the basic fighting position. (2) Begin a single jump forward by pushing off with your rear foot, leaving the ground and landing first on your front foot. (3-5) As soon as your rear

4

Front View

5

Front View

Side View

Side View

foot lands, execute a heel kick, being sure to follow through in the inward circular motion and making contact with the back of your heel.

Side View

Side View

Side View

133

JUMPING HEEL KICK APPLICATION

HAPKIDO DEFENSES

DEFENSE AGAINST FIST ATTACKS

The following techniques show the beginning student of Hapkido the various automatic defenses which can be used in fist attack situations. These techniques should be practiced until they become reflexive so that you will not have to think, but only react to an attack.

FIST ATTACK I

(1) Begin by facing your opponent in the basic fighting stance with your left foot forward. (2) When your opponent attempts to connect with a right punch to the face, step your front foot slightly outward and deflect his strike downward with

your forward hand. (3) Keep a grasp on the opponent's striking hand at the wrist, twisting your upper body with the punch. (4 & 5) Using the very same hand which deflected the attacking blow, execute a backfist to the opponent's face.

Front View

Front View

Front View

FIST ATTACK II

(1) Begin by facing your opponent in the basic fighting position with your left foot forward. (2) When your opponent attempts to connect with a right punch to the face, take a quick step back with your front foot so that you are in a right foot forward fighting stance, and deflect

Front View

Front View

Rear View

Rear View

his blow with your forward hand, which is now your right hand. (3) Maintain your grasp of the opponent's striking hand and twist your upper body along with his punch. (4 & 5) Using your deflecting hand, execute a right backfist to the opponent's face.

Rear View

Rear View

Rear View

Front View

Front View

Front View

FIST ATTACK III

(1) Begin by facing your opponent in the basic fighting position with your left foot forward. (2) When your opponent attempts to connect with a right punch to the face, step your front foot (the left, in this case) slightly outward and deflect the blow with the outside forearm of your rear hand. (3) Make a knife hand and cock your arm to the

Front View

Front View

Rear View

Rear View

opposite side of your head, twisting
your hips in the same direction.
(4 & 5) Execute a reverse knife
hand strike to the opponent's ribs,
remembering to utilize the twisting
of your hips in the same direction
for increased power. Be sure to
follow all the way through with the
strike.

Rear View

Rear View

Rear View

Front View

FIST ATTACK IV

(1) Begin by facing your opponent in the basic fighting position with your left leg forward. (2) When your opponent attempts to land a right punch, simultaneously deflect it with an outer forearm block, step forward and outward with your rear

Front View

Front View

Rear View

foot so that it is in front of your left foot and pointing at a 45-degree angle away from it, and raise your right hand in a knife hand. (3) Twist your hips to the left and execute a right horizontal knife hand strike to the opponent's neck.

Rear View

Rear View

145

Front View

Front View

Rear View

Rear View

FIST ATTACK V

(1) Begin by facing your opponent in the basic fighting position with your left foot forward. (2) When your opponent attempts a right punch, step back with your front foot and deflect the blow with your rear hand (right,

3

Front View

4

Front View

Rear View

Rear View

in this case). (3 & 4) Maintaining a grip on the opponent's striking hand, turn your hips to the left, place your weight on your left foot and execute a right side kick to the opponent's midsection.

Front View

Front View

Rear View

Rear View

FIST ATTACK VI

(1) Begin by facing your opponent in the basic fighting position with your left foot forward. (2) As your opponent throws a right punch, step back with your front leg and deflect the blow with your right hand (formerly

3

Front View

4

Front View

Rear View

Rear View

the rear hand). (3 & 4) Maintaining a grip on the opponent's striking hand, place your weight on your rear leg and execute a roundhouse kick.

FIST ATTACK VII

(1) Begin by facing your opponent in the basic fighting position with your left foot forward. (2) As your opponent steps forward and attempts a right punch, deflect it outward with your rear hand while you simultaneously step back with your front foot. (3) Follow through immediately with a right front snap kick to the opponent's abdomen.

DEFENSE AGAINST KICKING ATTACKS

The following section is meant to illustrate a variety of different counterattacks that you can employ against a kicking attack. These techniques will cover many different types of kicking attacks that can be employed against you and, as in the previous section, the defense techniques should be practiced until they become reflexive.

Front View

Front View

AGAINST THE FRONT KICK I

(1) Begin by facing your opponent in the basic fighting position with your left foot forward. (2) As your opponent attempts a right front kick, deflect it to the outside with your rear arm while you simul-

Front View

Rear View

taneously step forward with your front leg at a 45-degree angle. There should be about two shoulder-widths between your legs. (3) Execute a forefist to the opponent's face with your other hand.

Rear View

Rear View

Front View

Front View

Rear View

Rear View

AGAINST THE FRONT KICK II

(1) Begin by facing your opponent in the basic fighting position. (2) When the opponent attempts a right front kick, step your forward foot back behind your other foot and bring your rear hand under the kick to hook it. (3) Maintaining your grip, execute an instep kick with your forward

Front View

Front View

Rear View

Rear View

foot (the right, in this case) to the groin. (4) Following the kick, step your kicking foot straight down to the floor and follow through with a left forefist to the face.

AGAINST THE FRONT KICK III

(1) Begin by facing your opponent in the basic fighting position. (2) As your opponent attempts a right front kick, step your forward foot back behind your other foot and bring your rear hand under the kick to hook it. (3) Maintaining your grip, execute a roundhouse kick to the opponent's head and (4) follow through with a backfist by the same hand which had executed the hook.

AGAINST THE SIDE KICK I

(1) Begin by facing your opponent in the basic fighting position. (2) As your opponent atempts a right side kick, deflect it with your rear hand while you simultaneously step your front foot slightly forward and 45 degrees to the side. (3) Maintaining your grip of the opponent's kicking leg, execute a forefist into his kidney, and follow up with (4) your other fist to the head.

Front View

Front View

AGAINST THE SIDE KICK II

(1) Begin by facing your opponent in the basic fighting position. (2) As your opponent attempts a right side kick, deflect it with your rear hand while you simultaneously step your front foot slightly

Front View

Rear View

forward and 45 degrees to the side. (3) Maintaining your hand beneath his kicking leg, execute a right side thrust kick to the back of your opponent's knee.

Rear View

Rear View

159

Front View

Front View

Rear View

Rear View

AGAINST THE SIDE KICK III

(1) Begin by facing your opponent in the basic fighting position. (2) As your opponent attempts a right side kick, deflect it with your rear hand as

Front View

Front View

Rear View

Rear View

you step back with your front foot. (3 & 4) Cock your blocking arm and execute a backfist to the head of your opponent.

Front View

Front View

Rear View

Rear View

AGAINST ROUNDHOUSE KICK I

(1) Begin by facing your opponent in the basic fighting position. (2) As he attempts a right roundhouse kick, deflect it with your forward hand while stepping forward and outward 45 degrees with your rear leg. (3)

Front View

Front View

Rear View

Rear View

Immediately follow through on the deflection with a right instep kick to the groin. (4) Drop your kicking foot straight down to the floor and execute a right forefist attack from this position.

Front View

DEFENSE AGAINST THE ROUNDHOUSE KICK II

(1) Begin by facing your opponent in the basic fighting position with your left foot forward. (2) As your opponent attempts a right roundhouse kick at your head, deflect it downward with both of

Front View

Front View

Rear View

your hands getting a grip on it while you simultaneously step back with your front foot. (3) Maintain a grip of your opponent's kicking leg and execute a right roundhouse kick to his head.

Rear View

Rear View

DEFENSE AGAINST
ROUNDHOUSE KICK III

(1) Begin by facing your opponent in the basic fighting position. (2) As your opponent attempts a right roundhouse kick, step your rear leg all the way forward and block the kick with both of your forearms. (3) Catch the kicking leg with

your hands, and bring your forward foot around and behind the opponent's anchor leg. (4) Maintaining your grip on his leg, execute a leg sweep so that your opponent falls to the floor.

SELF-DEFENSE
TECHNIQUES

There are a number of Hapkido self-defense techniques which are helpful for use in emergencies. These techniques do not require a great deal of knowledge in the martial arts and thus, would be most useful for women who desire some kind of insurance against being accosted. All of the following techniques involve some form of contact, or in-fighting defense, with the man as the attacker and the woman as the defender.

SELF-DEFENSE I

(1) The attacker grabs you by the right wrist. (2) Still facing your attacker, free your right wrist by snapping your arm inward immediately after the attacker makes contact. (3) Step forward with your right foot and cock your right arm so that your

elbow points outward, level with your shoulder. (4) Execute a reverse elbow strike, hitting the attacker in the jaw with the point of your elbow after you have swung it in a circular and horizontal motion.

SELF-DEFENSE II

(1) The attacker grabs you by the right wrist. (2) Step forward with your left foot so that your hips are perpendicular to his and chop down on his elbow with your left hand, freeing his grasp. (3 & 4) Swing your body around to your right by stepping out and back with your right foot, and pivoting on your left. (5) As you pivot all the way around, execute a right elbow strike into the attacker's midsection.

Close Up

Close Up

SELF-DEFENSE III

(1) The attacker grabs you by the right wrist. (2) Using your other hand, grasp his attacking hand by the wrist. (3) Maintaining your grip, free your

Close Up

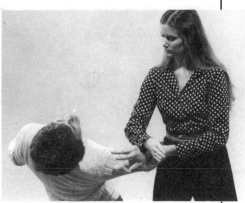

Close Up

other hand by pushing it forward and upward. (4) Still maintaining your grip, use both of your hands to bend his attacking hand backward at the wrist.

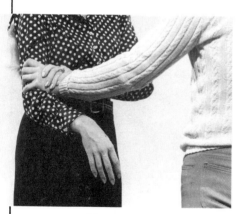

Close Up

Close Up

SELF-DEFENSE IV

(1) The attacker begins by grasping you with both arms at the elbows. (2) Move your left hand across your chest and grasp his left hand at the wrist, while you simultaneously raise your other hand. (3 & 4) Maintaining your

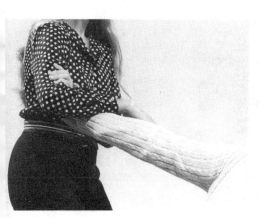

Close Up

grip on his left hand, swing your right arm over and down upon his left forearm.

SELF-DEFENSE V

(1) The attacker begins by grasping you around the throat with both hands. (2) Step forward with your right foot, grasp his upper body with your left hand and begin a right knife hand strike to his throat. (3) Complete the

knife hand strike by following through until your arm is extended, remembering to maintain your left hand grip. (4) Bring your left leg forward and execute an upward left knee strike to his groin.

SELF-DEFENSE VI

(1) The attacker begins by grasping at your neck from behind. (2) Pivot on your right foot and spin to your left, getting a view of the attacker. (3 & 4) Grasp

him around the back with your left arm and execute an upward palm strike to his chin, being sure to follow all the way through.

SELF-DEFENSE VII

(1) The attacker begins by grasping your left wrist from behind. (2) Pivot around on your left foot and turn your body to the left. (3) Continue the turn until your right foot is behind the attacker's

forward foot, and simultaneously execute an upward right palm strike to his chin. (4) Push forward with your palm strike and backward with your right leg, causing the attacker to lose his balance.

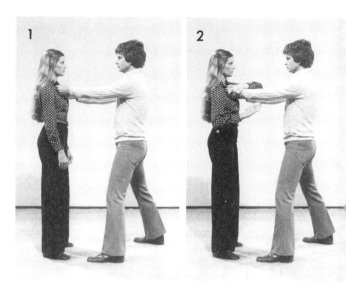

Front View

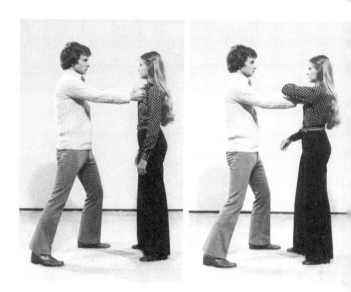

Rear View

SELF-DEFENSE VIII

(1) The attacker begins by collaring you from the front with both hands. (2) Bring your left arm across your chest and grasp the attacker's left arm at the wrist. (3) Grasp his same arm in front of the elbow with your right hand. (4 &

5) Maintaining both of your hand holds, swing your right elbow up and over his left arm and force downward.

Front View

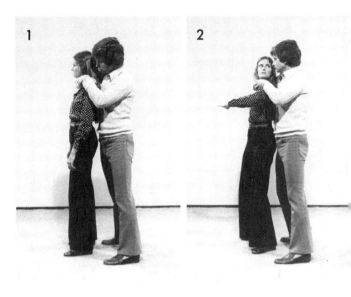

Rear View

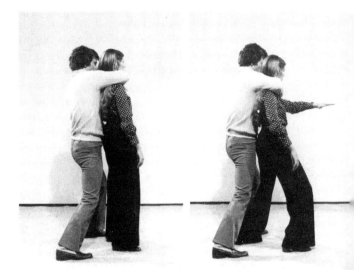

SELF-DEFENSE IX

(1) The attacker begins by executing a strangle hold from behind with his forearm. (2) Turn your head to the side to avoid strangulation and look toward his head as you cock your left arm inward. (3) Execute a left outward

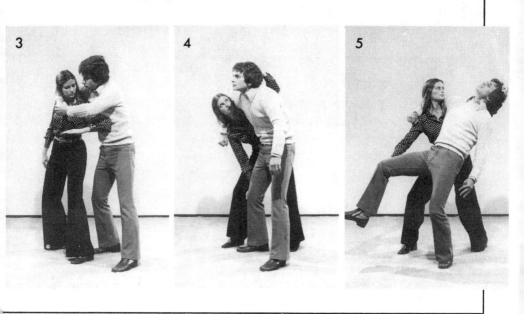

elbow strike in a circular motion to his ribs. (4 & 5) Grasp the attacker by the hair and behind the knee and pull the head down and the knee up as you straighten your body, causing him to lose balance.

Front View

Front View

SELF-DEFENSE X

(1) The attacker begins by attempting a strangle hold while he sits astraddle on you. (2) Execute an upward left palm strike to his chin. (3) With your other hand, grasp the attacker by the back of the head,

Front View

Front View

Rear View

pulling down with your right hand and pushing up with your left palm strike. (4) Continue exerting your hands in these directions until the twisting of the attacker's head obliges him to roll off you.

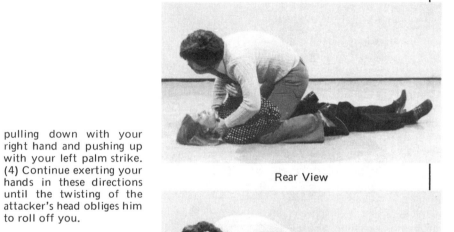

Rear View

Rear View

Rear View

SELF-DEFENSE XI

(1) The attacker begins by applying a bear hug from the front. (2 & 3) Grasp the attacker behind the head with your left hand

and execute a right upward fingertip strike to his face, being sure to follow through until he releases his grip on you.

TARGET AREAS

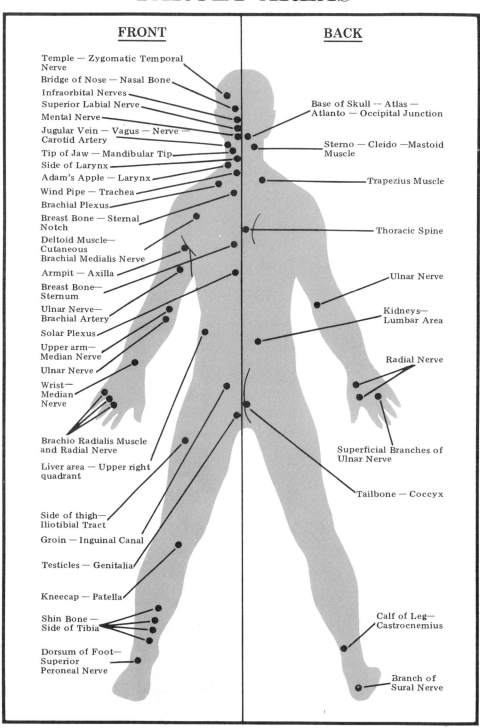

FRONT

BACK

Temple — Zygomatic Temporal Nerve

Bridge of Nose — Nasal Bone

Infraorbital Nerves

Superior Labial Nerve

Mental Nerve

Jugular Vein — Vagus — Nerve — Carotid Artery

Tip of Jaw — Mandibular Tip

Side of Larynx

Adam's Apple — Larynx

Wind Pipe — Trachea

Brachial Plexus

Breast Bone — Sternal Notch

Deltoid Muscle— Cutaneous Brachial Medialis Nerve

Armpit — Axilla

Breast Bone— Sternum

Ulnar Nerve— Brachial Artery

Solar Plexus

Upper arm— Median Nerve

Ulnar Nerve

Wrist— Median Nerve

Brachio Radialis Muscle and Radial Nerve

Liver area — Upper right quadrant

Side of thigh— Iliotibial Tract

Groin — Inguinal Canal

Testicles — Genitalia

Kneecap — Patella

Shin Bone — Side of Tibia

Dorsum of Foot— Superior Peroneal Nerve

Base of Skull -- Atlas — Atlanto — Occipital Junction

Sterno — Cleido —Mastoid Muscle

Trapezius Muscle

Thoracic Spine

Ulnar Nerve

Kidneys— Lumbar Area

Radial Nerve

Superficial Branches of Ulnar Nerve

Tailbone — Coccyx

Calf of Leg— Castrocnemius

Branch of Sural Nerve